Colorado's Geography

Joe Rhatigan

Table of Contents

Chapter 1

Regions of Colorado

Golden **prairies** stretch as far as you can see. Snow-topped mountains touch the sky. Deep **canyons** and towers of colorful stone grow into and from the earth. Can you imagine a place with all these things? It seems like a fantasy. But it exists. It is Colorado.

Colorado is a state in the western part of the United States. It is easy to find on a map. Why? Because it is a simple rectangle. It shares one corner with New Mexico, Arizona, and Utah. This is the only place in the country where four states meet in four perfect corners.

Colorado has three unique regions as part of its geography. They are the High Plains, the Rocky Mountains, and the Colorado Plateau.

Lines of Latitude and Longitude

Latitude and **longitude** are lines that form a numbered grid on a map. Latitude lines run east to west. Longitude lines run north to south. You can use these lines to pinpoint any place on a map. They are written like this: 39.7° north, 105° west. This is Denver's location.

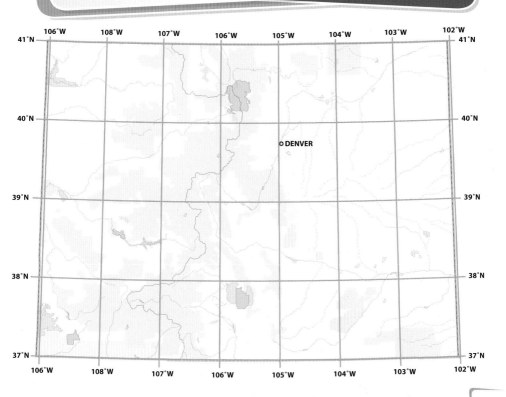

The High Plains

The High Plains cover the eastern part of Colorado. This part of the state is made up of grasslands without a mountain in sight. It looks a lot like Kansas, a neighboring state. The weather here is very dry. It is hot in the summer and cold in the winter. The soil is rich, and there is a lot of grass.

These conditions make the High Plains perfect for farming. Farmers plant crops and raise livestock. There are thousands of ranches and farms in Colorado. Many of them are in the **plains**. Most of Colorado's big cities, such as Denver and Boulder, sit between the High Plains and the Rocky Mountains.

Tornado Alley

Keep an eye on the weather forecast in the High Plains. The flat, grassy prairie is a hot spot for tornadoes. There are about 50 tornadoes every year in the state. They mostly happen in late spring and early summer.

The Rocky Mountains

The Rocky Mountains, or Rockies, are in the middle of the state. They are tall and grand. Fifty-eight of the peaks are huge. They reach 14,000 feet (4,267 meters) or more above sea level. These are called *fourteeners*. The Rockies pass through many states. But Colorado has its tallest peaks.

People love to visit the Rockies. They come to ski, hike, and explore. **Tourism** brings in a lot of money for the state. It brings in a lot of people too!

The Rockies run along the Continental Divide. This is an invisible line across the land. It runs from British Columbia to Central America. Rivers west of this line flow to the Pacific Ocean. Rivers east of it flow to the Atlantic.

Maroon Peak and North Maroon Peak

Pikes Peak

This peak is known as America's Mountain. It is a popular place for tourists to visit. It is also sacred to the Ute Indian Tribe.

Colorado Plateau

The Colorado Plateau is in the western part of the state. The mountains here have flat tops! These are called **mesas**. In Spanish, *mesa* means "table." The mesas rise above deep canyons. The largest mesa in the world is here. Grand Mesa soars 6,000 ft. (1,829 m) above the valley. It is 40 miles (64 kilometers) long.

The red stone here gives the state its name. In Spanish, *colorado* means "red." It also means "colorful." Parts of Arizona look a lot like this as well. The Grand Canyon there is *colorado* too.

The Colorado River runs through the **plateau**. It crosses six other states and part of Mexico too. Farmers grow fruit in the valleys of the plateau. And many fossils are found near the western border. Dinosaur National Monument is there. You can visit and see the fossils yourself.

Grand Mesa

This modern irrigation is based on the same methods used by the Puebloan peoples.

First Farmers

The Puebloan peoples lived here thousands of years ago. They were great farmers. They developed a system to **irrigate** the land. This means they invented ways to bring water to the plants. People who came after them learned from their methods.

Chapter 2

Geography's Effect on Colorado

The geography of a place shapes how we live there. People who live near an ocean might become fishers. People who live in a desert might conserve water.

But people also shape the landscapes we live in. We drain water away to clear the land beneath it. We use dams to control the flow of rivers. We build tunnels through mountains. We turn valleys into cities.

Each culture that has lived in Colorado has interacted with the land in different ways. They have worked with the dry **climate**, animal life, and fertile soil of the plains. They have used the resources of the mountains and mesas. These things are woven into their lives.

Big Stratton Reservoir

Resources Galore!

Colorado has many things that people need
or want. It has farmland and **fossil fuels**.
It offers wind and solar energy, gold, and
wood from trees. But these things cannot be
used without affecting the environment and
people. All resources should be used wisely.

American Indians

Humans have lived in Colorado for thousands of years. Long before people from Europe settled, many great American Indian nations lived here. These included the Ute Indian Tribe. The Utes were hunters, gatherers, and traders. Legend has it that they have lived here since the beginning of time.

Also here were the Apache, Comanche, and Shoshone peoples. The Cheyenne and Arapaho tribes lived here too. Each of these groups changed the landscape by how they lived. They made hunting trails. They diverted river water for farms.

The land, in turn, changed them. The native people moved when the weather got cold. Or they moved where hunting was better.

American Indians from many nations still live in the state.

Ute Indian Camp, 1913

The Ute Indian Tribe

The Ute people have three official tribes. The Southern Ute Indian Tribe and the Mountain Ute Tribe are in Colorado. The Northern Ute Tribe is in Utah. You can learn more about them by visiting their websites.

The Utes have two tribes in Colorado today. They were once nomadic. They did not stay in one place. So, they knew a lot about Colorado's geography. They were also experts on its plants and animals.

Each year, the Utes moved among different hunting and gathering grounds. This gave plants and animals time to **replenish**. The paths the Utes traveled were very useful. Later, European settlers used those same paths. Some trails, such as the Ute Pass, are roads today.

the Ute Trail in Rocky Mountain National Park

More native people began to move to the High Plains. This was so they could hunt **bison**. Bison thrived here because they lived off the grasses. Bison were very important for food, shelter, and clothing. Then, the tribes began trading bison hides to the settlers. They hunted bison at a faster rate to keep up with the demand. This led to near extinction. And it changed the landscape of the plains.

Mammoth Changes

There were once mammoths in the area. Scientists are not sure why they became extinct. They think humans may have over-hunted them. Or the climate changed.

Europeans

Gold has always been a big deal. The first Europeans came to Colorado to find gold. Spanish explorers came in the 1500s. But they did not find gold. It was too hard to find.

Rumors of gold in the Rockies led to a gold rush. The Colorado gold rush peaked in 1859. More than 100,000 gold seekers came to the area. They came from all over the country. They set up camps and forced the Utes off their land. Many stayed to form towns. In fact, two mining camps became the cities of Denver and Boulder.

Before mining, there were very few European settlers here. But they came for gold, and they stayed. The gold in the streams and mountains changed history! Mining remained an important part of the state's economy for many years.

burro train carrying gold ore down a mountain trail

Breckenridge, Colorado

Tourism Galore!

The whole state is popular with tourists. They come from all over to see the **national parks**, mountains, and mesas. Tourists ski, hike, and go rafting. They also visit the bustling cities.

Settlers forced the Cheyenne and Arapaho peoples off the plains with an 1867 treaty. The native people were faced with violence and starvation if they did not agree to it. The settlers then used the land for large cattle ranches. Later, they turned to farming.

The climate of the plains influenced these farmers. Lack of water led them to work together to create irrigation ditches to water their crops. When rain was plentiful, more people farmed. But when a major drought came, farms failed and people left.

The farmers used the land poorly. Their practices and the drought dried up the plains. This caused giant dust storms. The region came to be known as the Dust Bowl in the 1930s.

Colorado Farms Today

Farming is still important in the state. Some farmers practice **dryland agriculture**. They use only rainwater. In this way, they do not deplete water sources.

The Colorado River

The Colorado River begins in the Rockies. It used to travel to the Gulf of California in Mexico. But people built a dam. It changed the river's flow. They did this to bring water throughout the Southwest. The people in these states needed water to drink. They needed water for farming too. Today, the river is not always strong or full enough to reach the ocean.

As **climate change** happens, there is less rain in the Rockies. This means less water in the river too. The people in the state rely on the river. As the population grows, the state will need more water sources.

Cutthroat Survival

The official state fish is the greenback cutthroat trout. It got its name due to its red throat. This fish was once thought to be extinct. Scientists have worked to bring the cutthroat back to rivers and streams.

CAL

BA.
CA

This map shows some of the dams along the Colorado River.

WYOMING

UTAH

Green

Colorado

Shadow Mountain

Granby

Grand Valley
Price-Stubb

COLORADO

San Juan

Lake Powell

Glen Canyon

Lake Mead

Davis

Little Colorado

Colorado

Parker
Headgate
Rock
Palo Verde

Salt

NEW MEXICO

Imperial
Laguna

Gila

Gila

ARIZONA

SONORA

23

Chapter 3

Movement in Colorado

People make states and countries, but Earth makes their geography. Land and water features cross state lines. States can have climates and landmarks in common. In fact, Colorado has a lot in common with other states in the Southwest. They are linked by geography and by the movement of people, products, and ideas.

Today, fast and easy travel means that people are always on the move. They come and go from state to state. But throughout history, people have moved in and around Colorado as well. They have **migrated** here. They have explored, traded, and vacationed. Some people chose to move. Others had no choice.

satellite view of a section of the Colorado River

Bent's Old Fort

In the 1800s, Charles and William Bent and Ceran St. Vrain created a trading empire in Colorado. They were among the first to trade bison hides at a place called Bent's Old Fort. They did this with the help of American Indians in the area.

Across States

Colorado shares its geography with other states. A trip down the Colorado River would take you through six other states and Mexico. A climb across the Rockies would take you through five other states. A tour across the Great Plains would stretch into ten states in all. Canyons like those in the Western Slope can be found in nearby states too.

Even so, no other state is just like Colorado. It has its own story. And the height of its mountains is beyond compare. It is a climber's paradise! People visit the state to enjoy its many beauties. They come from all corners of the world. Many are willing to travel far to see its wonders.

Denver

Denver is the capital of Colorado. It is called the Mile High City. It has an altitude of 1 mile (1.6 kilometers) above sea level. Its economy relies on the transportation of goods to nearby states and cities.

Movement in History

In the early history of Colorado, many groups of people moved through its regions. The Utes moved in yearly cycles. This was so they could hunt and find shelter in the winter. The Comanche, Cheyenne, and Arapaho peoples settled here. They first came to the plains hundreds of years ago.

The first Europeans to come to the area were from Spain. They were followed by many others. They all found people already living in the area. But some claimed the land for their own.

Then, the United States bought a large piece of this land from France. This was called the Louisiana Purchase. It included a big portion of Colorado. Explorers found resources people wanted. These included gold, farmland, **game**, and more. Settlers soon followed. Miners came too. They forced the native people from their land.

the Louisiana Purchase territory

The Names We Know

American Indians named many places in the country. Some of these names are still used. Others have been changed. The mountain known as Pikes Peak was called *Tava* by the Ute Indian Tribe. The Arapaho people called it *heey-otoyoo'*.

Trade and Movement Today

People move to Colorado all the time. They come from other states and other countries too. Also, many tourists visit the state. As many as 86 million people visit each year!

Colorado's resources are also on the move. They move from one part of the state to another. And they move to other states and countries too. They are sold or traded for resources people need.

Here is an example. Wind power comes mostly from the eastern part of the state. The Colorado River is in the western part of the state. Water from the west is shared with the east. Energy from the east is shared with the west.

Colorado also exports goods to other countries. Some of its biggest exports are electronics and beef.

interstate highway in the mountains

A Legacy

Rodolfo "Corky" Gonzales was the son of an immigrant. His father came from Mexico. Gonzales worked for justice for Colorado immigrants. He was a well-known activist. But he was a famous poet and boxer too!

Living with Geography

Geography can be a tool for understanding the world. To live in a place, humans have to adapt to it. We work with the features of the land. We also change the land just by being here.

Sometimes, these changes have consequences we do not plan. Building a dam across the Colorado River created unexpected problems. So did farming that replaced the grasses of the plains with wheat.

The geography of Colorado helped create its history. And it will help create its future. What will that future look like? Will there be more **wind turbines** or coal? Will there be new paths to water? Will new resources be found? Whatever people decide, geography will play a role.

National Nature

The United States owns one-third of Colorado's land. Much of this land is made up of national parks. The public can visit them to enjoy nature.

NATIONAL PARK SERVICE

drone view of Golden, Colorado

Chapter 4

Mary Cronin: Master Mountaineer

Mary Cronin was born in Denver in 1893. The mountains were her home. But she was feeling bored with her life and looking for something new to do. She noticed an upcoming climb with the Colorado Mountain Club. This was a group of climbers who went on long and even dangerous hikes and climbs. Cronin fell in love with mountain climbing. She had to be part of this thrilling world.

Fairly soon, Cronin climbed her first fourteener. She climbed with Agnes Vaille. Vaille was a well-known climber. The two became close friends. They both wanted to join the "14,000-Footers Club." This was the group of people who climbed all the state's fourteeners. At that time, no women and just a few men had done it.

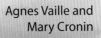

Agnes Vaille and
Mary Cronin

The Colorado Mountain Club

The Colorado Mountain Club began in
1912. It brought together people who love
mountain climbing. The club still exists!

Tragedy struck in 1925. Vaille climbed Longs Peak in the winter. No one had ever done this before. But a storm struck. Vaille never made it back down.

Cronin was heartsick at the loss of her friend. But she was determined to go on. She became a leader among climbers. In 1925, she climbed five fourteeners in three days! She was also the first woman to reach the top of Lone Eagle Peak. Then, in 1934, she climbed her last two fourteeners. She had achieved her goal!

Cronin became the first woman in the 14,000-Footers Club. And she became a climbing legend for all time.

Longs Peak

For the Lady Mountaineer

In the 1800s, it was rare to see a woman who wore pants. Women climbed mountains in dresses or the flannel bathing suits of the day. By Cronin's time, pants were more accepted.

Lone Eagle Peak

Cronin Peak, named for Mary Cronin

Glossary

bison—a large animal with short horns and shaggy mane, related to cows and oxen

canyons—deep valleys with steep cliffs on both sides

climate—the average weather conditions of a region over a long period of time

climate change—a change in the average conditions (such as temperature and rainfall) in a region over a long period of time

dryland agriculture—the practice of growing crops without the use of irrigation

fossil fuels—natural fuels, such as gas or coal, that were formed millions of years ago from the remains of living things

game—animals that are hunted

irrigate—to bring water to crops

latitude—the distance north or south of the equator measured in degrees

longitude—the distance east or west of the equator measured in degrees

mesas—flat-topped mountains with steep sides

migrated—moved from one country or region to another

mountaineer—a mountain climber

national parks—areas set aside by a country's government to preserve the natural environment

plains—large expanses of flat dry land

plateau—a high, level piece of land

prairies—grasslands

replenish—build up again

tourism—the activity of traveling to a place for pleasure

wind turbines—tall towers with blades that use wind power to produce electricity

Index

Geography in Your Community

Learn about your area's geography. How does the geography affect what jobs people have? How does it affect what tourists do? Has the landscape been changed to make things easier for people to live there?

Use your research to create a brochure. In it, tell about your community and its geography. Here are some ideas to get you started:

1. Fold a sheet of paper in thirds to create six panels.

2. On the cover panel, include an image that best captures your community. Add a snappy slogan.

3. Inside, describe the natural features and tourist spots your community offers. Include images.

4. Include quotations from a few residents about why your area's geography is so great.

5. On the back panel, create an ad for your favorite geographic spot in your community.